JOURNEY FROM SOUL TO SOUL

LOVE NEVER ENDS

KUSHAGRA BANSAL

This book is dedicated to Mr. Rohan Shah.

This book is dedicated to Mr. Rohan Shah.

Contents

Contents

Foreword

" A man of many thoughts and skills
And of many words and some that kills"
" A man with style on the street
A soul so spiritual and sweet"
"A man with natural talent and rhytm
Which is obviously sacred and god given"
" A man who creates dish with spice
A cuisine that taste so nice"
" A man so learned and young
A song that will always be sung"
" A man who's god is knowledgeable and so dear
Who he knows will always be near"
"A man of passion and sometimes fear
Who's life is just getting in to gear"
"A man who is partial to a drink and smoke
Who always drink his whisky with coke"
" A man of honour,verve and of tradition
With a dream and ambition"
"A man with a devine smile
You just have to start for a while"
A man in body and in name
But who's path is just not the same"

Neil Andrew Robinson

Educator & Photographer

Preface

This book is all about that divine feeling called love. This book can tell you what can happen when you fall in love with someoneWhat if someone suddenly leave you on your own. So basically this book is so much melancholic in one way and motivational in another way.

Acknowledgements

1. If you try

"One try give me hope

One try makes me happy"
But,

"One try brinfgs new light in life
I wish people understand the value of one try"

Because,
"One try brings the smile on those faces
Who never smile since you left"

Just one try

Think about it

2. My Life

"I burn my heart in coals, Never let my love fade"

"That's all i want my only wish was
May my breath get shelter in your heart"

"Let me cry, Atleast i am having that right still, Let me swell oth
of my eyes,
There's so much pain"

"My tears are telling my story, Not strong enoufgh to hide them
anymore"
"Now you should tell me should i die, Or live with this painful
moment"

"But, don't worry i will not give up, Till my last breath"
"Ever green leaves come on a dry tree, I hope happiness will come
in my life too"

• 3 •

3. Games

"Now many games, I win already
I am loosing the battle of love life"
"No matter how many lamps i light,
The lamps doesn't light up life"
"This time is very strange,
Work, anger and greed, I can leave easily"

"If i want to, How can i forgot you my beloved"
"You don't know what you are for me,
I see you how the heart melts"

"Your love is also a bond,
You should tell
How can i free myself
Still there's a river of love
Let me be your and only your helmsman
Let's sail together my soul mate"

4. Half Moon

"Half moon shines in that hope

That will complete one day"

"I smile in that hope,

That you will complete me one day"

5. I Miss

"I miss those days, We spent together"

"I hug those pictures, We clicked together"

"If my destiny is to apart from you"

"Then i will comeback,

Like the springs comeback after a beautiful winter weather"

6. Regrets

Yes, i have regrets, My eyes are red and wet"
"You will come back to me, That i can bet"

"Will get very little time with you, That's my biggest worry till yet"

"Yes, i need you every hour and every second,
And need to hold you in my arm,
Whole day and just chat"
"I love you so much darling,
Just hug me and don't be upset"

7. My eyes

"Look in to my eyes, These eyes always cry"

"Listen to my heart, Almost going to die"

"Falling in love with you, But, It's time to say good bye"

"Still saving some breaths for you, I don't know why"

"Don't bother my love and,
Don't ask me why"

8. Birds and me

"Birds can fly with wings,

Same with love"

"A person can love someone,

Only from heart, Not with their brain"

9. Complication

"I remember our old conversation' You just remember our
complication"
"I always want a good relation, Now you will say, It's over
expectation"

"I am really tired of all these things,
Let's resolve our issue and give this relation a new acceleration"

"I am empty from inside,
What just left is our memories and guilt of lack of
communication"

"It's all up to you now, Leave me like this or come back to me"

"Take it as a beautiful invitation"

"I love you so much my darling,
You are my only motiation"

10. Book

"Life is just like a page of a book
Its just a calculation of a profit and loss"
"And love is a book on its own

If its happens then they can write their book on their own"

"The only thing precious in love
And that's your love"

"In that mostly people don't understand ,
How precious it is"

"And, Those who understand
But can't fulfill them"

11. I love you

"Life is neither in today nor in tomorrow
For me life begins when I am with you"

"And stops when I am apart from you, Without you a single day is
like a year
When I meet you I got confused what to wear"

"My destiny is already decided, That I am going to be with you"
"But still asl me that am I okay without you,

I know I cant see you,, I know I cant call you,
I know I cant text you"

"No matter where are you, With whom are you"
"But I know I love you"

12. Insomniac

"Now a day you make me insomniac, When I will go for forever
Than I don't want you to become insominiac, But that's not my
purpose to go,

My only purpose to go, is just to complete my sleep whenever I go,
Please don't miss me in nights, Because I love nights"

"When I open my eyes after I cry, And I see the sunlight with
some beautiful twilight"
"Then I start writing on you, After switching on my night light"
"And start with the first moment, When we just met under the
street light"

13. Die

"Now a days I prefer to die, Rather than cry
Because you said me goodbye"

"And you know I cant live without you, And the reason you give
me is I smoke that's why"
"When I tried to ask you something, Before speaking I sigh"
"I just want to hug you last time, Before I gonna die"

"That's all I wish
Before my soul fly
But still sacrifice
And walk away from you
Yes I am gonna die"

14. Can i see you again

"May be I never see again, All the moments are flowing like rain"
"Your eyes touch me, That's all I gain"
"Yes I still love you rather than pain"
"I always want you to be free, Rather than putting you in chain"

"I travelled all the way, Just to see you
Just by train"

"But still wish that
To see you again"

15. Why

"Why you pray daily for me
If you don't love me"

"Why you miss me
If you don't love me"

"Why you keep my pictures
If you don't love me"

"Because, I know you love me"

16. You are to me

"*You are important to me*
As melody is important for a composition"

"*You are in me*
As lyrics are to a song"

"*I feel you,*
Just like a musician feels the rhythm"

"*I cant be completed without you*"
Just like the composition cant be completed
Without a beautiful melody"

17. Everything

"Every doubt brings stress,
Every dream brings hope just like,
Every springs brings flowers for me,
Everyday brings me near to death"

18. Love with book

"As books look beautiful in a glass cupboard"
"But its actually more beautifully to read them
Same with love"

"Its look beautiful in seeing or listening virtually"
"But in reality its only the experience of it,

That is divine"

19. It will not be me

"Try anything to kill me
Use any knife on me"

"Do everything to hurt me
Go anywhere you want to go without me"

"But the only thing I can say from me
The last words will be your name
When my soul leaves my body"

"Don't ask me to comeback
It will not be me"

20. Whatever

"Whatever you will say to leave

I will

"But don't ever say to leave you"
"Wherever you will say to go"

We will

"But don't say to go on my own"
"Whatever you wish I also will"
"But don't wish to apart from me"

21. Ink and words

"*I wish that the day pass, After my eyes blink*"
"*Don't know what brings me near to you, I don't know what that link*"

"*I always feel you everywhere, When I write about you*"

"*No matters whats the color of the ink*"

"*I love to kiss you, Yes,I still remember*"

"*The color of your lips was pink*"
"*No matter where I am And always think*"
"*I just want to hug you, Because that moments is always distinct*"

22. Rhyme

"I cried a lot without you from my tears"
"Still cant believe you believe in"

"Strangers thoughts what they
Say in your ears"
"I know you been upset on your own"
"that's what I know"
"That's why I comeback to let you back
Into your comfortzone"

"Now its time to resolve everything
I know you want to talk about manythings"

"I promise you ,I will never let you down on anything"
"But please trust me this time,
That's the only reason ,I write this beautiful rhyme"

23. No matter what

*"No matter how big and deep the trunk of the tree is,
Even the ray of sun crosses it"*

*"Same with love,
No matter what comes to you,
But don't stop loving someone"*

24. Travelled

" *I travelled but the destination was you* "

" *My heart was broken but you were the reason of my heart beat* "

"*Today there is no journey no destination*
But still you are the reason for living"

25. Home

"*I called it home for you its just a bunch of bricks*"

"*I called it bouquet for you its just a formality*"

"*I called It love for you its just a lust*"

26. Feel

"They never demand never expect"

"Finding the right one not on love"

"Because love is not the topic to read"

"It's a feeling to feel"

27. What is love

"One similarity between love and dreaming"

"Anything can happen in these both"

"No boundaries and No limitations"

28. Trip

"All this trip without you is just like rain"
"Some people say, I am insane"

"All I feel is just me and my pain, I attend all the meetings and just faint"

"Not interested in profit and loss, Its just your love that's what I gain"

"Never care about anyone else, For me its just you that's what I main"

"Without you all the moments are full of strain, Realise the life without you is full of chain"

29. Killed by you

" *I drink that poison*
If served by you"

"*I accept any challenge*
if host by you"

"*I welcome that death from my open arm*
If I killed by you"

30. Online

"When you are online,did you ever know, How I feel,when i didn't get any sign"

" Days and days passes, I keep seeing your profile picture in that hope,
That today you will reply, But now what I thought was just fake hope"

"Today your profile picture changed, But what about me no hope and no change"

"You enjoy your every single day, But I am still there in that hope that
Your one reply will make my day, Understand the value of people before they changed"

"No point to understand the value when the soul fly ,
And choose different body and than its all changed"

31. Can i stay in your life

"Is there any way ican stay in your life,
Don't say no, I dint want to cut my wrist from knife"
"How can I be so blind in love with you,
Where I cant see no right nowrong only just you"

"Cant be bother about me anymore,
You already turn me into you'
I don't need any sympathy any attention,
What I need is just only you"

"People say stars are watching us ,
What if I become the stars and watching only you"

"I know this path is not having any destiny,
Didn't care about any destiny anymore"
I know this path is you and I will always choose you"
When I am not here with you read this poem,
And I will alwaye be with you"

32. You

"I always talk to the stars about you there is no stars today,
You tell me whom I talk today about you"

"Crying on my own and just missing you"

"I want to do everything just to talk to you"

"I am fully broke and realize all my faults,
And what I did with you"

"Please forgive me ,I want to be with you"
"Please forgive me ,I want to be with you"

33. Alive

"Walking while carrying sleep in my eyes
Still I am alive"

"Carrying pain in my heart
Still I am alive"
"A hope of meeting you in my heart
Still I am alive"

"Carrying all your infedility in my heart
Still I am alive"

"Fighting with whole society just for you
Still I am alive"

"If I gone for forever, remember I will always alive in you
Yes, still I am alive"
"Still I am alive"

34. GOOD BYE R....

"*Counting my last breath, But still waiting for you*"
"*Having last supper with my friends,*
But, Don't want to go for forever just for you"

"*Keeping apart these emotions,*
Wish you could understand how much I love you"

"*Don't come on my funeral,*
I don't want to see you"
"*I don't want to see you*"

SOAR to *Success*

by Mastering the ART of Organizing Information to *Finally* Get Things Done!

by Andrea Anderson

CEO Productive Environment Institute
with Barbara Hemphill, Author of Taming the Paper Tiger

Published in the United States of America by

Spirit Media and our logos are trademarks of
Spirit Media Inc
205 Academy Street STE 3251
Cary, NC 27519
1 (888) 800-3744 | https://spiritmedia.us

Business & Money | Skills | Time Management

Paperback ISBN: 979-8-89307-207-5
eBook ISBN: 979-8-89307-209-9
PDF ISBN: 979-8-89307-208-2
Library of Congress Control Number: 2026900275